On Show at Exhibitions and

An illustrated guide for those staffing stands at exhibitions or hosting in hospitality suites

by

Sarah Turley & Veronica Shutes

illustrated by

Jan Herbert

Greenfield Publishing

This book is dedicated to:

**All our colleagues who inspired this book.
Those who didn't get it quite right!**

First published in Great Britain in 1995 by:
Greenfield Publishing
P.O. Box 12,
Kenilworth,
Warwickshire, CV8 1ZS

Printed and bound in Great Britain by:
Gecko Print Limited
Bicester, OX6 7PP

ISBN 0-9523-3281-7

Acknowledgement

This book is based on an idea first originated by the authors when employed by THORN EMI Electronics. They are grateful to the Company for permission to exploit the idea in this publication.

CONTENTS

INTRODUCTION

This booklet has been produced to help and guide those who work at exhibitions and in hospitality suites. It examines what is needed in staff terms for a successful and smooth running event.

It recognises that stands and suites, like companies, come in a variety of sizes. The basic rules are the same regardless of the size of the event or the company. The variations range from a large stand with purpose-built rest and storage areas, and a large staff under a trained manager, to a small booth with no privacy and minimal staff.

The same variety applies to hospitality suites, which may be associated with an exhibition, stand alone, or shared with other companies. Regardless, enthusiasm for the event, teamwork and over-riding consideration for the customer are the essential ingredients.

THE STAND

General

Working on an exhibition stand, particularly during a long show, can be tedious and extremely hard work. All staff must co-operate as a team; there is no room for individualism.

Professionalism is also vital. Potential customers very quickly see through bluster and lack of knowledge.

All staff must work to promote the company image and ensure that they use the stand to the greatest possible advantage. This is best achieved by careful staff scheduling with no more than half a day's continuous duty.

... like show business ...

Exhibitions are pure show business

Attendance at an exhibition is a hugely expensive advertising production. As such it must be used to maximum advantage to reap the best return from the investment.

All staff should act in a professional manner, avoiding the temptation of high spirited behaviour. Their standards reflect the image of the company.

Prior to the opening, staff should familiarise themselves with the layout of the stand, the schedule of attending personnel and the location of all essential services.

Hello, got any logo-bugs?

The stand is your shop window

This is where you display your goods or services and the reputation of your company can be made or lost. There is never a second chance to make a good first impression.

Treat all-comers with the same courtesy, even if instinct tells you that there is no apparent advantage. Today's time waster could be tomorrow's customer or even a member of a customer's family.

All areas of the stand must be kept clean and tidy; clear of dirty cups, ashtrays and junk mail.

Do you present the right image?

Personal standards

Vast amounts of time and money are spent on designing and building the stand. You should take as much care with your own appearance.

Company name badges and clothing should be worn if available. This helps identify you to customers.

Please dress smartly; nothing outrageous. Try to get a good night's sleep. Tiredness and hangovers show you at your worst.

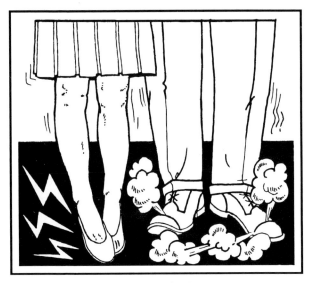

Feet on fire?

Wearing tight shoes

The state of your feet is reflected in your face. Shoes should be smart but above all else comfortable. Try to break-in at least two suitable pairs well in advance of the show. A change of foot-wear halfway through the day provides relief to swelling ankles and groaning toes.

Try to rest your legs horizontally during off-duty periods. Other useful ideas to minimise discomfort, especially in hot weather, are to use mineral water aerosols or 'cologne wipes'.

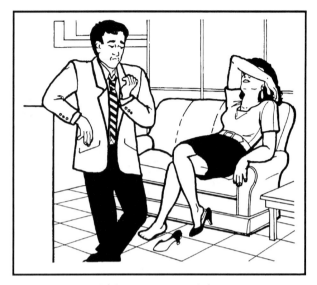

Wishing you weren't here

You are not invisible on the stand

After several days on the stand both exhaustion and boredom set in; a strange feeling of transparency overwhelms.

However, you never do become invisible. You are on view the whole time, so if the desire to collapse or scratch becomes too great, please retire somewhere out of sight.

You're not just there to stand and leer ...

The exhibitor's leer

Exhibitions seem to turn some perfectly normal sales staff into ogling idiots. With the addition of loud verbal accompaniments, it presents a very down-market image.

It could be that the ogled person turns out to be a customer who might take offence.

Smoke, alcohol fumes & bad breath

Oral vices

Smoking, drinking or eating on the stand looks un-
professional, can be quite offensive to some visitors
and leaves unsightly debris. Bad breath and the odour
of garlic can be minimised by good oral hygiene and
the use of mints.

On large stands, refreshments can be provided in the
storeroom, the ideal place for a quick puff, gulp or
munch. Those less fortunate on smaller stands should
find a restaurant or move away from the stand for
the occasional cigarette. These restrictions, however,
must not be imposed on visitors to your stand.

How do I deal with them?

The initial contact

It is essential to build a quick rapport with visitors. Think about appropriate visual, verbal and physical approaches, particularly with overseas visitors. When demonstrating equipment, three possible phrases give completely different results:

- Let me show you. It's really interesting.
- It's fully backward compatible and upgradeable.
- Please don't touch.

Avoid the hackneyed question "Can I help you?" Introduce yourself and shake hands. Initiate the conversation with "What is your particular interest?"

Whatever you do, do not stalk, hover, avoid, or pounce on visitors to the stand.

Sorry, I can't remember what it does.

Know your products

Visitors come to find out about your products, systems or services. It is vital that you are fully conversant with them, can demonstrate equipment where appropriate and have answers ready for all eventualities.

It is also important to be 'five minute survivable' on those exhibits on the stand which are not your direct responsibility.

If you are caught out with an awkward question, admit you do not know the answer, promise to find out and always ensure that someone does respond.

The right-handed fluggle valve works a ..

Baffling technicalities

It is easy to get carried away describing the technical intricacies of your product or system but you might be blinding your audience with science. At best they stop listening, at worst you drive them away.

Emphasise the benefits and advantages. Keep it simple until you can gauge the depth of explanation required.

Well, I think it's ... I'm not sure.

Who's in charge

A senior person from sales and marketing should be available at all times to deal with any issues which do not come within the remit of the stand manager.

All stand staff should be aware of who is undertaking this role and who is the stand manager. These two are responsible for the smooth and efficient running of the stand. This fact should be accepted by all other staff.

He went that away ...

Houdini

It is essential that the stand manager knows who is scheduled to be on the stand and where they are during the day if they have to leave.

When you leave the stand, inform the receptionist or the stand manager of your contact point and your estimated time of return.

Pagers or mobile phones are the answer to exhibitors' prayers. Use them if you have appointments in several different places or are otherwise un-contactable.

'm ... er ... I'll try to find one of the directors.

Dealing with VIPs and the Press

Plan any VIP visits to the stand in advance. Such people, by definition, rarely arrive unannounced though not necessarily on time. Press visitors need similar care as the company is always 'on the record'. Everyone must know the 'party line' on contentious issues.

A senior member of the company should be available to welcome these visitors and escort them around the stand. Such tours must be pre-planned to view key items of likely interest.

VIPs usually operate to very tight schedules, so lengthy detailed presentations are a non-starter. Concentrate on a summary, in layman's language, of benefits and specific points of interest.

Get the form filled in

Brochures and enquiry forms

Control of literature is important. It is essential to know the details of the recipients to enable the leads to be followed-up after the exhibition.

No genuine potential customer will be reluctant to give a business card or address when asking for a brochure.

The list of names gives an opportunity to gauge the success of the event. Control also stops competitors and other free loaders picking up copies of your costly brochures.

I'm sure I've got one somewhere!

Running out of business cards

Better a surfeit of cards than too few. It is amazing how many you will use during the course of an exhibition and there is nothing more embarrassing than running out.

Exchanging cards at the end of a conversation ensures you have the full name and address of all your contacts.

Isn't he from Competeco?

Competitors

Try to identify any visitor before engaging deeply in conversation. Competitors use various guises to do market research. Keep an eye open for familiar competitor faces. Get them off the stand quickly and politely.

Conversely, it is always useful to gather as much information as possible from competitors. For this task, choose people who are:

- Unknown to the competitors
- Not wearing any company identity
- Able to provide convincing answers
  if asked for whom they work
- Not on duty

It's for you

The office

Stands and hospitality suites are not extensions of your office. Receptionists, no matter how willing to help, do not have time to act as secretaries.

If you have to catch up with urgent office work, outside secretarial help is usually available at larger exhibitions, but remember it can be expensive and may not be commercially secure.

You'll never guess what happened next ...

The phone hog

Telephones are the only lines of communication between the stand, any associated hospitality suite and the company's office, occasionally supported by fax. It is vital that these lines are open at all times.

Please keep calls to a minimum. If it is essential that your life story is dictated to the office, please use public telephones or a mobile.

Is there anybody there?

Packed stand

A particular problem for large companies is groups of visiting employees congregating on the stand. The resulting congestion this causes is a real deterrent to potential customers.

Day visitors from the company should be actively discouraged from lingering on or near the stand. There is plenty for them to do; size up the competition and look for new developments at the show.

Got somewhere I can stash these, luv?

Left luggage

Stands and hospitality suites always have limited storage space. Avoid bringing unnecessary baggage to the exhibition unless absolutely necessary.

You can always leave your briefcase, coat or umbrella in your car, or at your hotel if you are staying near the exhibition.

Your lunch box, suh!

Hazardous material

As with luggage, do not bring a briefcase to the exhibition. You will not need it, as the stand is not an office substitute.

If you do find life too difficult without it, please limit the size to a document case and ensure that it is clearly and visibly labelled. Store it in the space available with the prior knowledge of the stand manager.

Any unlabelled item is likely to be treated as a potential threat and disposed of accordingly.

Order form

To obtain further copies of this book or the floppy disc of briefing material, please complete and return this form, together with a cheque made payable to:

Greenfield Publishing
P.O. Box 12
KENILWORTH
Warwickshire CV8 1ZS

Please mail me:

.... packs of 5 copies of *On Show at Exhibitions & Events* @ £35.00 per pack including postage & packing.

.... 3½" floppy discs containing briefing material @ £15.00 each including postage & packing.

.... copies of *Winning Major Business* @ £35.00 incl. post & packing. Quantities of 5 or more @ £30.00 each.

I enclose a cheque for £ ....

Name: ....

Job Title: ....

Company: ....

Address: ....

....

....

Postcode: ....

Please tick box if a receipt is needed

Available from Greenfield Publishing

Winning Major Business is a ground-breaking book. It provides new ideas and practical approaches on marketing and selling to governments and other institutional purchasers. At last, a major text is available dealing with the specialised field of winning large contracts.

For the newcomer to the subject, and those facing the challenges of a recent promotion, it will provide a ready reference and accelerate their progress in this complex area. **The experienced** will be able to revise their knowledge and review recent developments.

The book will be of interest to those supplying the aerospace, construction, defence, electrical & electronics, instrumentation, information technology, machinery, process control, public utilities, telecommunications and transport markets.

Alex Weiss has spent thirty years in a variety of sales and marketing roles in the UK electronics industry. Stephen Willson combines eleven years of marketing in North America with wide experience of industrial training. He is the principal of Marketing & Commercial Development, a company providing custom-designed training in industrial marketing.

Business Age says: *"... a serious but readable explanation ... the book breathes."*

The Marie-Celeste syndrome

The eleven-thirty lunch rush

If you are on duty on the stand and have to act as a host for lunch at the hospitality suite, it is essential that you are in the suite before your guests arrive.

However, before leaving the stand, ensure that your exhibits are 'covered' by someone else. Also check that the individual left on the stand is comfortable with your exhibits, is fed, watered and has had a chance to inspect the plumbing.

Elevenses

Visiting vultures

On large stands, amongst the other delights of the rest area, sandwiches and other light snacks are sometimes supplied for those working on the stand. This can help to alleviate the interminable queues in over crowded restaurants for warm beer, cold coffee and curly sandwiches.

If you are just a daily visitor from the company, or if you are lucky enough to be hosting in the company's hospitality suite, please do not use the stand staff's hard-earned lunch as your hors d'oeuvre.

THE HOSPITALITY SUITE

Introduction

A hospitality suite, whether associated with an exhibition or some other social or sporting event, offers customers mid-morning coffee, lunches, afternoon teas or alcoholic beverages. Pleasant surroundings encourage business discussions or just socialising. When applicable, it also provides adequate viewing space to watch relevant displays, events or competitions.

Whether the company approach is to provide an informal buffet or a formal dining arrangement, the service provided by catering staff should be as swift or relaxed as appropriate. Speed is crucial at popular events where 'second sittings' may be necessary in a formal situation.

At the start of each day, a meeting should be held with scheduled hosts to discuss details and prepare for all eventualities. Every day should be taken as it comes and the predominant message is the need for flexibility.

Keep calm and carry on

The receptionists

Receptionists are the first point of contact for guests to a company hospitality suite. Their most important asset is the ability to remain calm and smiling while:

- Checking in guests and issuing their badges
- Booking their belongings into a cloakroom
- Filtering them through to meet their hosts in the main area of the hospitality suite

They are not however employed to act as personal or social secretaries to company hosts.

Crisis? What crisis?

Reception

Always greet guests as soon as they arrive, welcome them and match them to their hosts. A good suite manager and pre-event preparation really make a difference.

Working in reception is not easy, particularly at peak times. The reception area must be kept clean and tidy; clear of cups and dirty ashtrays.

A good supply of pens and notepads should be available, together with a full first aid kit. A notice or pin board is needed for messages for customers and company staff.

Miss LaBelle is my personal assistant

Guests

Customers come in many different guises, requiring flexibility and versatility:

- The perfect one on the right day
- The near-perfect, who was due yesterday, but could only come today
- The imperfect, with an uninvited colleague
- The disaster, who turns up in place of someone else who has already refused the invitation with regrets

Remember, all customers are equally welcome and must be accommodated, but beware of smooth-tongued gate-crashers seeking a free meal.

Be prepared

The potential hosts

Hosts' behaviour must be impeccable, welcoming and courteous. Ensure you have the latest acceptance lists, enabling you to plan your days. Be in the suite ahead of your guests to avoid embarrassment.

Hosting is an art. For some it is natural, for others it is difficult and has to be acquired. Be subtle. Introduce business only after a few niceties. Listen to customers to find out what they want. Never overpower them with work. They might actually want to watch the event.

Remember not to complain directly to the catering staff if you have a problem. Instead, speak discreetly to the suite manager.

Where am I hosting?

The selected hosts

As host, you must know your guests' names, if not their faces, to avoid awkward list checking. Familiarise yourself with their cultural norms and dietary needs to avoid giving offence. Also heed the risks of mixing guests from unfriendly organisations or nations.

Allowing guests to 'wander' alone gives an uncaring impression. Despite warnings about punctuality, a roving host is essential and everyone should look out for lonely guests. Make them welcome and try to match them to their host.

Groups of hosts ignoring guests creates the worst impression. Always circulate, helping colleagues wherever possible.

The Lunch Lurker

The extra host

Not every nominated host may be needed each day, particularly in hospitality suites located at major exhibitions. Attend the morning briefing meeting to establish whether your presence is required.

If not needed, stay away from the suite. This also applies to visiting employees who feel it is their right to have a free lunch on the company.

Keep a cool head in the face of adversity

Calamities

A steady drip from a leaking roof, floods from a deluge, an infestation of ants, power cuts or general damp are all problems for tented hospitality suites in the some climates.

Most can be dealt with on arrival at the suite; others require an immediate reaction. Some call for mopping up operations and placating the unlucky victim with the least possible fuss.

Whatever the calamity, the message is 'keep calm, be tactful and diplomatic.'

Bombe Surprise?

The threat

A bomb scare must be regarded seriously. If requested to leave the hospitality suite, it is essential to vacate it as quickly and quietly as possible. The manager will be in overall charge of the evacuation.

The same is true in the event of fire and in either case, no attempt should be made by anyone to collect belongings from reception.

Five year plan? I'll give 'em five year plans.

Meetings

The hospitality suite manager needs to know the dates and times of any meetings arranged by company staff, in order to organise tables and provide light refreshments.

Separate meetings must not be arranged to occur during the preparations for a meal or during the meal itself.

Well, how about a week Friday?

Communications

Telephones in a hospitality suite are for general use and not for personal business or arranging the social calendars of company staff. Ideally, one should be reserved for incoming calls only.

Company employees who need either to make frequent telephone calls or to be continually available should equip themselves with a mobile phone.

A girl's got to look her best

The facilities - Ladies

Ladies, please leave the cloakroom as you would wish to find it.

We aim to please. You aim too, please.

Gentlemen

Gentlemen, need we comment further?

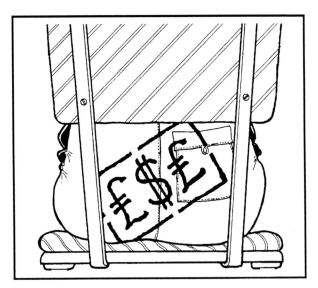

Price per seat

Conclusion

The provision of a friendly atmosphere, with the flexibility to cover all contingencies, is an expensive operation. It is up to those on duty to ensure that the money is well spent on the furtherance of business and continuing customer goodwill.

SURVIVAL KITS

General

Whatever the venue, survival kits are essential. They should be equipped to deal with all possible eventualities. Furthermore, at least one person should be a trained first-aider. The following lists are easily adaptable to cover any event from large-scale international exhibitions to attendance at small sporting events.

Although full documentation should be distributed to staff prior to the event, always ensure that the items shown in the following lists are available.

Event documentation

- Entrance tickets & car park passes
- Blank business cards & name badges
- Guest badges
    - complete & blank
    - distinguishable from staff badges
- Up-to-date guest acceptance list
- Complete invitation list with job titles
- Stand staff & hosting schedules
- Schedule of visiting delegations
- Literature request forms
- Company, emergency & site services phone numbers
- Details of local restaurants & hotels

To survive needs skill and preparation

For Stand and Hospitality Suites

- First aid kit (including items for a hangover, headache or stomach upset)
- Stationery (headed paper, envelopes, pens, note/ 'Post-it™' pads, stapler, drawing pins, etc.)
- Notice board
- Emergency cleaning equipment (small vacuum cleaner, dusters, anti-static spray, polish, etc.)
- Shoe-cleaning kit
- Business gifts, company ties etc.
- Emergency sewing kit including safety pins
- Electrical maintenance kit & extension cable
- Rubbish bags
- Backup tapes/software if video/computers used

Additional items for Hospitality Suites

- Hosting schedules
- Visitors' book
- Cloakroom tickets
- Coat hangers
- Menus

Facilities

At large exhibitions and events, there are often private ladies' and gentlemen's cloakrooms. A good supply of the following items is essential:

- Roller towels or paper substitutes
- Soap
- Disinfectant
- Loo rolls
- Tissues
- Air fresheners
- Cleaning materials

Whatever the event, the message is:

"Always be prepared"

EXHIBITION MANAGEMENT

Whether to go

No book about exhibitions can be complete without looking at some of the issues facing company management. By far the most important is whether to exhibit at any particular show. The following questions need careful consideration.

- Why have we chosen this exhibition?
- What is the expected attendance?
- What message will we try to convey?
- What are we going to exhibit and how?
- How should we judge our success?
- How large a budget can we afford?
- Which staff should attend?

It is assumed that a public relations specialist will be responsible for organising the design and build of the stand and hospitality suite, to a brief provided by the marketing function.

It is important to make a prompt start with the compilation of the event invitation list, since a good response from potential guests will only be achieved if the invitations are sent early.

Don't decide on attendance purely by location

Selection of Staff

The people who are responsible for the smooth running of the event must be selected carefully. They should be team players and au fait with a majority of the company staff. They must be keen to do the job even though it may mean unusual working hours and only short breaks, if any.

Stand and suite managers should know the company, its product range and customer base. They should be unflappable and above all, pleasant, friendly and professional.

Receptionists must be selected for their ability to work in a team, talk to customers and smile sweetly through any adversity.

An exhibition or event is not the place for emotions, personal problems, not liking other staff or sulking. For these reasons, it may be preferable to use professional receptionists from reputable agencies rather than internal staff.

Hosting requires special skills that must be recognised in the selection of suitable staff for the role. Those who find difficulty initiating conversations with strangers should not be chosen. Particularly with overseas guests, it needs a subtle approach, starting with niceties and eventually broaching the topic of business. For many, hosting is a skill which has to be learned, and both training and feedback are important if the standard is to be improved. Above all, hosting needs to be recognised for the hard work it actually is.

The company sales & marketing lead is particularly important in dealing with the hosting of visiting VIPs and providing briefings to all staff at the start of each day. Senior directors should always be encouraged to attend exhibitions and other events.

Dying on your feet

Length of duty

Stand managers — remember if you want exhausted staff on the stand, assign them whole days back-to-back for a week. Working at an exhibition involves spending unusually long periods standing up, and talking to customers is never a relaxing occupation.

The duty roster needs careful preparation to ensure the right staff are available. It is essential that details are communicated to all those named, and the relevant managers.

Briefing agenda

The importance of briefing all staff attending any exhibition or event cannot be over-emphasised. For large companies attending major events, a formal briefing a week in advance has a number of advantages in terms of getting the message across. Where only small numbers of people are involved, a short informal meeting can quickly cover all the salient points.

- Name, location, date(s) and official opening times of the event
- Time staff are required to arrive
- Company aims at the event
- List of invitees and VIPs
- Level of company involvement, including items of equipment being exhibited
- Stand and/or hospitality suite layout
- Staffing schedule and eating arrangements
- Names of key event managers and their roles
- Hotel, travel and car parking arrangements
- Standards of dress and name badges
- Entry tickets

The information given should always be backed by a printed document for reference.

In addition, it is advisable to hold a pre-event or, if multi-day, a daily morning meeting, prior to the opening of the exhibition or event. Discussion should include a brief on any visiting VIPs and delegations, any problems encountered on the previous day, daily hosting schedules and any other relevant issues.

Post-mortem

It is not easy to judge the success of attendance at an exhibition. The gut feel, while usually correct, is a qualitative rather than a quantitative assessment. It is therefore important to consider such factors as the number of:

- Enquiry forms
- Visitors to the stand
- New sales leads
- Occasionally, confirmed sales

A debrief after the exhibition is important if stand staff and managers are to learn from their experience. Feedback of the quantitative performance is helpful in terms of future motivation. A video camera, as well as recording the stand for posterity, can be used to highlight any weaknesses found in the performance of staff on competitors' stands at the show.

Follow-up

All enquiry forms should be evaluated and the appropriate response action taken - a letter, fax or telephone call, together with any requested literature or information. It is critical that everyone who has completed a serious enquiry form should receive a suitable reply from the company.

The briefing disc

To enable effective briefings to be given to those involved in exhibition duty, and hosting at events or in hospitality suites, a 3½" floppy disc is available, in a self-contained IBM PC format, based on the contents of this book. It contains a number of view graphs of key messages, including illustrative cartoons, which may be printed out using a PC and copied onto view foils for use at briefings.